FIGHTING FOR CHANGE

For permission requests, write to the below address:

PYP Academy Press
141 Weston Street, #155
Hartford, CT 06141

The opinions expressed by the Author are not necessarily those held by PYP Academy Press.

Ordering Information: Quantity sales and special discounts are available on quantity purchases by corporations, associations, and others. For details, contact the author at tycwriter@gmail.com.

Edited by: Gary Hoh, Kassandra White
Cover, typeset, and formatting design by: Nelly Murariu
Illustrations by: Vijay Char
Additional Designs by: Mack Hoh-Choi

Printed in the United States of America.
ISBN: 978-1-955985-28-4 (hardcover)
ISBN: 978-1-955985-27-7 (paperback)
ISBN: 978-1-955985-29-1 (ebook)

Library of Congress Control Number: 2021921213

FIGHTING FOR CHANGE

Andrew Yang's Path Forward

Maddon Hoh-Choi & Tina Choi

Illustrated by Vijay Char

This book is dedicated to
Philip Choi, our beloved
father and grandfather,
who taught us to
always move forward
no matter what.

As a five-year-old boy, Andrew Yang knew that America could be an even better country.

But he had to wait 40 years before he was able to share his vision with millions of Americans. He did it by running for President of the United States.

In 2020, Andrew became the first Chinese-American to run for President in the 21st Century.

In 1975, Andrew Yang was born in Schenectady, New York.

He grew up in the small town of Somers, New York. Its neighborhoods had white clapboard and brick houses, and American flags were proudly displayed in the front yards. The summer days were hot and humid, and the winters had freezing temperatures.

Living in this small town, young Andrew noticed that not many people looked like him. Somers had very few Asians.

Andrew's parents came to the U.S. from Taiwan in the 1960s, and they met in college when they both attended the University of California in Berkeley.

They both believed in receiving a good education, and they taught Andrew about the importance of hard work and perseverance.

His mom, Nancy, was great with numbers and earned advanced degrees in math and statistics. She was also an artist who read to young Andrew from beautiful picture books about inspiring world leaders, like Dr. Martin Luther King Jr.

His father, Kei Hsiung, had an advanced degree in physics. He became an engineer and obtained 69 patents for General Electric and IBM.

While at home one day, young Andrew saw an Asian face on television.
He shouted out, "Mom! Mom! Look, that man looks like me!"

His mom said, "Andrew, do you think he is Chinese, Japanese, or Korean?"

Andrew grinned with happiness and replied, "I don't know,
but he looks like ME!"

His mom said, "It doesn't matter.
We are all in America now, and
he worked hard to be on American TV."

Andrew remembered
her next words
for years to come:
"Work hard, and you
can be anything!"

"It was inspiring to finally have a role model. Andrew made it possible for me to dream."

—Eric Quach, on being part of Yang's Movement

It was moments like these that became important to Andrew because they motivated him to make his parents proud.

Andrew didn't go to kindergarten—instead, he went directly to second grade, at only five years old!

Even though he earned the right to be in his class, he often felt like he didn't belong with his classmates. The other kids were taller and bigger. Andrew was always the smallest kid, and being Asian, he always looked different.

But Andrew always remembered his parents' words on perseverance.

"My mother hammered into me, anything someone else can do, you can do too."–Andrew Yang

Andrew was a very bright student growing up. He was especially strong in English vocabulary because he loved reading comic books.

He challenged himself to get good grades and do his best on tests.

It was like a game for him. Just like video games, he wanted to get the high score.

Andrew studied so hard and was so gifted that at 12 years old, he took the Scholastic Aptitude Test (SAT) and scored 1,220 points out of 1,600. That's a good score for anybody, but especially for someone who is 12!

(Most people don't take the SAT until they are 15 or 16 years old.)

Welcome, Andrew

SAT
May 5, 1987

1220
Total Score

640
Evidence-Based Reading and Writing

580
Math

View Details

Throughout school, Andrew's classmates bullied him. They called him slurs like "banana head," "gook," and "chink."

He vividly remembers when his school had an International Day. Andrew proudly brought in food from his own culture: a rice cooker filled with fried rice.

But his classmates ridiculed him.

During both elementary school and junior high, Andrew was often ignored or picked on simply because of his ethnicity. Kids made fun of his eyes and said he was ugly. Andrew was upset because he believed it was fundamentally wrong for him—or anyone—to be treated that way. Andrew defended himself and always stood up for what he thought was right. He knew people should treat one another better.

It hurt to be made fun of, but Andrew didn't let the bullies stop him from studying hard.

While he was working hard in school, Andrew would tell his mom,

"I really don't care about the grades. But I know you want me to get As, so I will get As for you."

He truly wanted to make his parents proud through all of his hard work.

Eventually, he earned a spot in a program for gifted kids, called The Center for Talented Youth. The program is run by the prestigious Johns Hopkins University, and Andrew was in it for five consecutive years.

During his time there, he learned even more and made friends with other talented students.

Andrew didn't just study at school. On Sundays, instead of playing basketball all day with his friends, Andrew rode 20 miles in his parents' minivan to attend Mandarin language class. The Mandarin Chinese language is difficult to learn, and this class was the one class in which Andrew struggled. The Chinese characters were strange, and sometimes they didn't make sense to Andrew. However, he knew his parents wanted him to learn the language and study the Chinese culture.

His frustration drove him to tears at times, but—as always—he persevered.

Andrew didn't only focus on
studying while he was growing up.

**Though he was a very
bright student, he was
also good athlete.**

As Andrew grew bigger, he
started to compete with other kids
in sports. He played tennis and
even joined the wrestling team.

In high school, Andrew's interests were typical of a 1980s American teen: new wave music, pro wrestling, skateboarding, comic books, and video games. His favorite games were Street Fighter II and Dungeons & Dragons.

He was also on his high school's drama team.

All those hours spent in role-playing games helped him become a flamboyant performer. He auditioned for his school's play and got a role as a professor.

In the 1980s, when Andrew was a teenager, many Americans were prospering. The Cold War with the Soviet Union was over, and Americans no longer felt scared about nuclear war. Not only did the country feel more safe, but technology was becoming more readily available. Just 10 years earlier, nobody had computers in their home, but now millions of families did. But despite America's prosperity, problems were growing. Political policies at the time lowered tax rates, so people could keep more of their income. This sounded like it would help, but these policies mainly helped the wealthy. Social programs were also cut, and many regulations that helped shoppers, employees, and the environment were eliminated.

By the time Andrew was an adult, he could easily see the problems that these policies created in America.

During this time, many people in America were succeeding — but many others were not.

Andrew always remembered his feeling of not belonging, and they motivated him to fight for change. Like a college professor, he wondered: How could the world be more fair?

He remembered his mom reading to him about equality and recalled the words of people like Dr. Martin Luther King. **"I Have a Dream!"**

When it was time for college, Andrew chose to study economics and political science at Brown University, a famous Ivy League college in Rhode Island.

After he graduated from Brown, he attended Columbia University in New York City in order to earn a law degree.

Though he graduated and became a lawyer, he was very unhappy with his job and quit just five months later.

Andrew felt terrible for leaving the path that his parents created for him. His parents' lessons about perseverance had never left him.

So he mustered the courage to create something by himself and succeed.

Andrew had always wanted to build something of his own. He started a few companies, but some failed. Despite this, Andrew wasn't going to give up.

In 2009, he achieved his first big success by becoming the Chief Executive Officer of a college preparation company called Manhattan Prep. He grew the company larger and larger, until it became the #1 test prep company in the United States. Even though he had setbacks in the past, Andrew had finally built something that was a success.

A year later, a big company called Kaplan bought Manhattan Prep. That made Andrew a millionaire.

Despite his wealth, Andrew didn't feel content. Not everyone in America was doing well. He knew that many of the young people who had worked for him needed help.

He asked himself:

Who could help solve some of the biggest challenges for America's cities?

Andrew reunited with his college friend, Charlie Kroll, who was an entrepreneur in New York.

Charlie encouraged Andrew to remember all the college graduates that he had trained at his last company. These people became an inspiration for Andrew.

In 2011, Andrew created Venture for America, a nonprofit organization that connected the smartest, most talented college graduates with startup companies.

With his new organization up and running, Andrew spent the next six years training college graduates to build companies that create economic opportunity in American cities.

"Andrew Yang's motivation is to help people." - Charlie Kroll

Venture For America

During this time, Andrew married Evelyn Lu, another Columbia University graduate who became a business executive. They had two sons, Christopher and Damian. Christopher was born with autism, a medical condition that requires special attention from the family.

Evelyn quit her well-paying job to take care of Christopher. Andrew saw how hard Evelyn's new job was. She was taking care of their children, planning doctor visits, managing the household, cooking meals, and performing many other tiring duties at home.

She had a difficult but significant role. **Andrew realized how unfair it was that the world did not see value in Evelyn's work.**

Though she didn't work in an office, Evelyn did have an important job!

While Evelyn worked at home out of the public eye, Andrew was receiving much recognition.

In 2012, President Barack Obama named Andrew a "Champion of Change" for his work with Venture for America. President Obama had created the Champions of Change program to honor ordinary Americans who were doing extraordinary work in their communities.

Three years later, Andrew met President Obama again when he was named as one of the Ambassadors for Global Entrepreneurship, a group that helped create more companies in America.

"To all the young entrepreneurs out here — you are the face of change."
– President Obama

2011
Champion of Change

Andrew's honors from President Obama energized him to do even more.

Meeting the President twice had been an inspiring experience. Obama's words were imprinted in his mind: "Andrew, we are in a fight to protect our middle class. And we can do that, but we must invest in the talent of our youth."

Andrew truly felt that his mission in life was to do something larger than himself.

Andrew continued to study and lead research on topics that would help Americans live better, have good jobs, and gain economic equality.

He wrote his first book in 2014 called *Smart People Should Build Things*. He wanted more Americans, especially new college graduates, to become entrepreneurs.

Based on his research, Andrew believed he knew how Americans could live better: through a plan for Universal Basic Income or UBI. With UBI, the United States government uses tax revenues to give every American adult citizen $1,000 each month to help end poverty.

If there was UBI in America, people would have the money to pay for basic necessities, like food, shelter, and clothing. They could find jobs to support themselves, pay off medical bills, and not worry about becoming homeless.

Plus, the $1,000 each person would get would almost immediately be spent, so that money also would help the economy, which helps everyone.

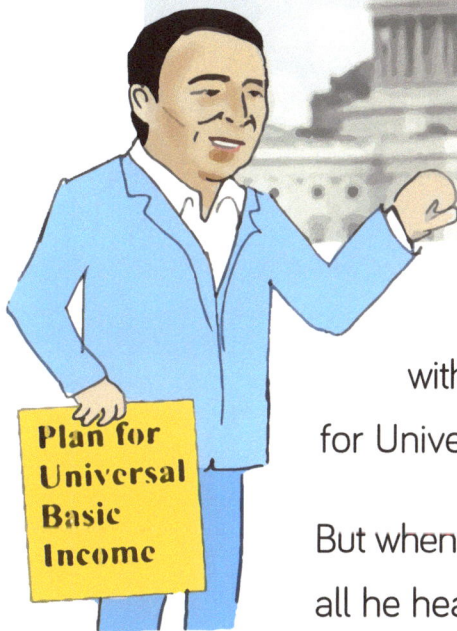

Andrew went to Washington D.C. to talk with politicians about poverty and to advocate for Universal Basic Income as a solution.

But when he finally got to talk with a Congressperson, all he heard was laughter. "Free money? No, that's never gonna pass. It's crazy," they told him.

It seemed like nobody in the government wanted to listen to or even cared about his ideas. But Andrew didn't give up. He asked himself how he could convince people to support UBI.

If government officials thought UBI was a crazy idea, Andrew would try another crazy idea: He would run for President of the United States.

At first, Evelyn thought he was just being silly, but he was serious. Evelyn embraced his plan, knowing his commitment to UBI and humanity was real.

In 2020, Andrew Yang officially became a candidate for President of the United States, and Universal Basic Income was the centerpiece of his campaign.

He made history again. He became the first Asian-American man from the Democratic Party to run for President.

Though he ran as a Democrat, Andrew wanted to help all Americans. Some politicians had used the slogan "America First," but Andrew believed in helping everyone. He used the slogan "Humanity First."

"It was inspiring to finally have a role model. Andrew made it possible for me to dream."

- Eric Quach, on being part of Yang's Movement

VOTE 2020

Andrew traveled all over the United States to meet people and hear what needed to be improved. This meant that he was often away from Evelyn and his two boys — which made him very sad.

Andrew knew, however, that to improve society, he had to get his message out to Americans.

He held rallies and made speeches to tell people about his plans. He talked to many interviewers from diverse news media and went on podcasts to discuss his message of equality for all.

He participated in seven of the eleven Presidential Debates and argued for his Universal Basic Income proposal. At one of the last debates, which was televised on TV, he was the only person of color there — just like in his childhood.

During his campaign, more people started to notice Andrew Yang and talk about him. People everywhere — North, South, East, and West — agreed that something needed to be done about economic inequality.

Andrew's common sense ideas and platform spread through news channels, the internet, and social media.

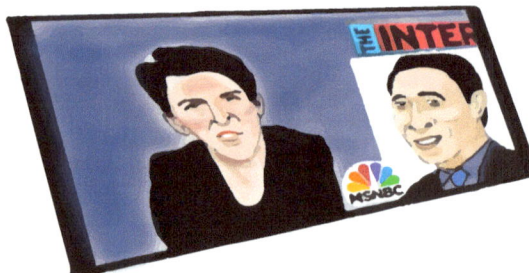

@andrewyang

@andrewyang

More than 1.6 million people supported Andrew, and called themselves the "Yang Gang." On social media, people posted news about him with #YangGang. His voices for humanity were being heard across America.

"It's great to see someone who looks like me running for President." – Eric Quach, Social Media Director of Humanity for Yang

Though Andrew was serious about solving problems, he also had a sense of humor. As the only person of Chinese descent in the presidential campaign, he tried to think of something that would highlight his uniqueness in a fun way.

He thought back to his childhood when there was a stereotype that Asians were "supposed" to be good at math. Andrew worked hard in every subject, but he WAS good at math!

$$+ - \times \div$$

MATH

Make **A**merica **T**hink **H**arder

With great pride, he told Evelyn his newest slogan would be "MATH: Make America Think Harder." He would put MATH on all his campaign hats to parody another candidate's slogan — it was hilarious!

Andrew really did try to make Americans think harder. He demanded common sense solutions, like saving taxpayers' money by eliminating the penny. He argued that you can't buy anything today with a few pennies. It costs more than 1 cent to make a penny, and people waste time needlessly when making change.

Andrew did not win the Democrat party nomination, and Joe Biden won the election, becoming the 46th U.S. President. However, Andrew Yang highlighted many issues, such as joblessness, poverty, and UBI, and brought them into the political discussion.

His new organization, Humanity Forward, is dedicated to helping politicians implement UBI and help families get financial aid.

Andrew always remembered his mother's words and persevered to make things better, even when people said terrible things about him.

Andrew inspired many Americans to aspire for more. He empowered Asian Americans, blue collar and white collar workers, truck drivers, tech workers, and people from all walks of life to follow his footsteps for change.

Andrew and his wife, Evelyn, continue to advocate for families who have children with special needs. Andrew Yang's courageous voice inspires millions of people across the country to fight for a better future.

"Andrew Yang truly brings everyone together through his inclusive leadership. He does not attack but fights for everyone. I highly respect him."

– Andrew Ly, Co-Founder and CEO at Sugar Bowl Bakery, Chair Emeritus Asian Pacific Fund

GLOSSARY

autism • a developmental disorder that restricts one's emotions and abilities

blue collar worker • a working class person who performs manual labor

political • relating to the government or the public affairs of a country

poverty • the state of being extremely poor

stereotype • a widely held, but fixed over-simplified image or idea of a particular type of person or thing

UBI • a government program in which every adult citizen receives a set amount of money on a regular basis

white collar worker • a person who performs professional, desk, managerial, or administrative work

CREDITS

Authors	Illustrator	Editors/Designers
Tina Choi	Vijay Char	Gary Hoh
Maddon Hoh-Choi		Mack Hoh-Choi

Maddon Hoh-Choi ✽ Many kids grow up watching sports and following their favorite athletes. Maddon grew up following politics and politicians, and he learned to recite the list of U.S. presidents like a baseball lineup. He founded the Civics Leadership Club at his high school, is a Bill and Melinda Gates Foundation Youth Ambassador, and a Civics Unplugged Fellow. Maddon believes in giving back to the community and was awarded a gold medal President's Volunteer Service Award. When Andrew Yang ran for President of the United States, Maddon finally saw a candidate who looked like him. Like Yang, Maddon wants a better future for the next generation. He has a dog, Brandy the Maltipoo, and three olive egger chickens. One of his favorite activities is running voter registration drives.

Tina Choi ✽ Born in Hong Kong and raised in California, Tina is the CEO and Founder of Travonde, Inc., an organization with a mission to strengthen communities and enrich the lives of older adults. An MBA graduate from Cornell University, Tina spent more than a decade with Apple Inc. in global operations strategy roles. She worked on Apple's most iconic products, such as the iPod, iPad, and iPhone, winning several awards for her work. She chaired the Apple Asian Association and championed many Diversity and Inclusion initiatives, including the Apple Entrepreneur Camp. Tina is mom to two children: Maddon and Mack. She believes representation in society matters, especially for younger kids.